Food and Festivals

A Flavour of FRANCE

Teresa Fisher

WAYLAND

Other titles:

Cover photograph: A market trader in Antibes, selling peppered salami and other cold meats.

Title page: A girl and her brother picking bunches of grapes in a vineyard in Provence.

Contents page: A float in the Nice Carnival parade.

First published in 1998 by
Wayland Publishers Limited 61 Western Road,
Hove, East Sussex, BN3 1JD, England

© Copyright 1998 Wayland Publishers Limited

Find Wayland on the Internet at http://www.wayland.co.uk

Series and book editor: Polly Goodman
Designer: Tim Mayer
Picture researcher: Shelley Noronha

British Library Cataloguing in Publication Data
Fisher, Teresa
   A Flavour of France. – (Food and festivals)
   1. Cookery, French – Juvenile literature
   2. Food habits – France – Juvenile literature
   I. Title
641.5'9 44

ISBN 0 7502 2220 4

Typeset by Mayer Media, England.
Printed and bound by EuroGrafica, Vicenza, Italy.

CONTENTS

France and its Food

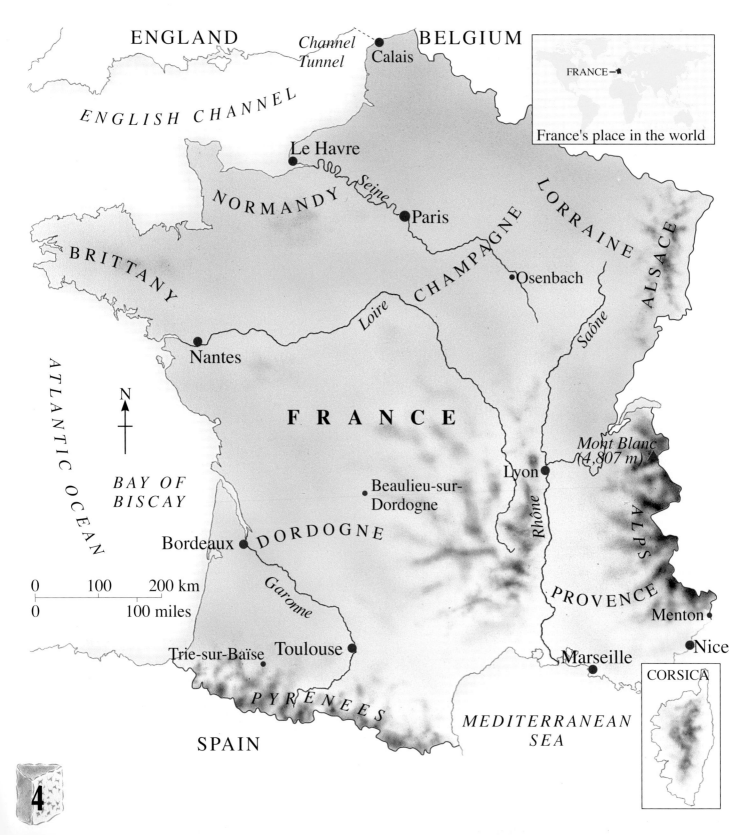

ENGLAND

Channel Tunnel

BELGIUM

Calais

ENGLISH CHANNEL

FRANCE →

France's place in the world

Le Havre

NORMANDY

Seine

Paris

LORRAINE

ALSACE

BRITTANY

CHAMPAGNE

Loire

Osenbach

Saône

Nantes

FRANCE

ATLANTIC OCEAN

N

BAY OF BISCAY

Mont Blanc *(4,807 m)*

Lyon

Beaulieu-sur-Dordogne

Rhône

ALPS

DORDOGNE

Bordeaux

Garonne

0   100   200 km

0   100 miles

PROVENCE

Menton

Trie-sur-Baïse

Toulouse

Marseille

Nice

PYRÉNÉES

CORSICA

SPAIN

MEDITERRANEAN SEA

4

CHEESE

Nearly every region of France produces its own special type of cheese. There are over 365 types in total. Many, such as Brie, Camembert and Roquefort, are famous all over the world.

WHEAT

Wheat is one of France's largest crops. It is used to make French bread, which is bought freshly baked every day.

FISH

French people eat lots of different fish and seafood, including plaice, sole and turbot from the English Channel, shellfish from Brittany and sardines from the Mediterranean.

VEGETABLES

Many different vegetables are grown throughout France. Onions, shallots and garlic are essential in French cooking. They add a strong flavour to many dishes.

FRUIT

The most important fruits are apples to produce cider, and grapes to produce France's famous wines. Apricots, cherries, strawberries, melons, peaches, oranges, lemons, plums and pears are also favourites.

OLIVES

Black and green olives grow in southern France, during the long, Mediterranean summers. Many are crushed to make olive oil, which is used for cooking.

Food and Farming

France is the largest country in Western Europe. It is famous for its fashion, perfume, fine wines and its *haute cuisine* (high-quality cooking). French dishes are always prepared with the freshest, tastiest ingredients available. Lots of garlic, herbs and spices bring out the flavours.

FROGS AND SNAILS

Have you ever eaten frogs' legs? In France they are a delicacy. They taste surprisingly like chicken and are delicious served with lots of parsley. Another delicacy is snails, which are eaten piping hot, straight from the shells.

▼ Frogs' legs don't look very pretty, but once they are cooked, they're delicious.

Well-known dishes include pâté (a paste of mashed meat or fish), *quiche Lorraine* (egg and bacon tart) and *coq au vin* (chicken and wine casserole). A popular fish dish is a soup called *bouillabaisse*. In the mountains, cheese fondue (chunks of bread dipped in hot melted cheese) is always a fun meal.

This chef is ▶ preparing a traditional soup, called *bouillabaise*.

Farming

France has more farmland than any other country in Western Europe. This means that French farmers can produce most of the fruit and vegetables, cereals, meat and dairy products that the country needs. French people do not have to buy much food from abroad.

▼ A grape harvest on a vineyard near Bordeaux.

▲ Villagers in Provence gather in an olive grove before their olive festival.

▲ Black and green olives are a tasty snack.

Different crops grow best in different regions. In the south, where the climate is warmer, the region of Provence is well-known for its olives, tomatoes, fish, herbs and citrus fruits. Western France, which has more rain, is known for its fruit and vegetables.

Cheese and dairy products

▼ This man is holding a round of Brie, which is a soft, creamy cheese.

In northern France, the fertile pastures are ideal for grazing cows. Normandy is famous for its dairy products, such as milk, cream and cheese. France produces enough types of cheese to eat a different one every day of the year. Many places, such as Livarot in Normandy, even hold special cheese festivals.

Livarot cheese is one of France's oldest cheeses. It is soft and creamy, with a reddish-brown rind and quite a strong smell. At the annual Livarot Cheese Festival, the locals wear traditional costumes, and there is singing and dancing.

Markets

The best time to buy local food in France is on market day. Most towns and villages hold their market day in the main square, once or twice a week. Large cities, such as Paris and Marseille, have fruit, vegetable and fish markets every day.

TRUFFLES

Truffles are a very rare kind of underground mushroom, which are about the size of golf balls. They are highly prized for their flavour. Truffles are sniffed out of the earth by pigs on leads, then sold for high prices at local markets.

Local farmers sell fresh fruit, flowers, vegetables, meat, eggs and cheese, and special local foods such as walnuts, honey, herbs and truffles.

▲ Truffle hunting with a pig in Dordogne.

This market trader is ▶ holding peppered salami, which is a favourite French delicacy.

Christmas

Most people in France belong to the Roman Catholic religion. One of their most important festivals is Christmas, the birthday of Jesus Christ.

Christmas celebrations in France begin on 6 December with the Festival of Saint Nicolas, the patron saint of children. You may know Saint Nicholas better as Santa Claus, or Father Christmas.

▼ It's fun when Santa Claus comes to town!

In some towns, a man dressed as Saint Nicolas rides through the streets on a donkey, and hands out sweets and gingerbread biscuits to the children.

Christmas Eve

On Christmas Eve, which is on 24 December, families get together for a special meal, called *Le Réveillon*. It usually starts with oysters, smoked salmon or *foie gras* (a delicious duck-liver pâté). The next course is turkey with chestnut stuffing, roast potatoes and many different vegetables. The food is washed down with a very expensive, fizzy white wine, called Champagne.

▲ Many different dishes are prepared for the feast of *Le Réveillon*.

If anyone is still hungry, there is the Yule Log, which is a rich chocolate cake in the shape of a log. It is coated in a creamy chocolate, vanilla or coffee icing sugar. There is a recipe for a yule log on the next page.

PROVENCE PUDDINGS

In Provence, for dinner on Christmas Eve, fish is more popular than turkey. But the best part of the meal is the dessert – thirteen different puddings, including dried fruits (raisins, figs and dates), nuts and nougat, cream cakes and clementines.

▲ A traditonal Yule Log, with miniature Christmas decorations.

Yule Log

EQUIPMENT

Chopping board
3 Bowls
Sieve
Wooden spoon

Round-ended knife
Fork
Christmas-cake decorations

INGREDIENTS

50 g Bar of chocolate
2 Teaspoons coffee essence
100 g Soft butter
200 g Icing sugar
1 Roll-shaped sponge cake (Swiss roll)

1

Break the chocolate into a small bowl. Stand it in a larger bowl, half-full of hot water. Stir until melted. Add the coffee essence.

2

Put the soft butter in another bowl. Gradually add the icing sugar through the sieve, and beat with the wooden spoon until creamy. Beat in the chocolate and coffee mixture.

3

Put the sponge roll on the chopping board and spread the mixture over it with the knife.

4

Use a fork to make stripey marks like bark. Decorate the log with Christmas cake decorations.

Festival of Kings

The *Fête des Rois* (Festival of Kings), on
6 January, celebrates the time when three
kings visted Jesus and gave him presents of
gold, frankincense and myrrh. In France,
this festival is the day when families
and friends give Christmas presents
to each other.

For tea on the *Fête des Rois*,
everybody eats a special cake,
which contains a lucky charm.
If you find the charm in your
piece of cake, you become
king or queen for the day and
wear a crown.

Queen for the day ▶
on the *Fête des Rois*!

Mardi Gras

Mardi Gras is carnival time in France. It is an ancient festival celebrated in Catholic countries on Shrove Tuesday, at the end of February or the beginning of March. Shrove Tuesday is the day before Lent begins. In the past, it was forbidden to eat meat or other animal products during Lent. So Shrove Tuesday, and Mardi Gras, was a day to eat up any surplus supplies in the house.

Today, Mardi Gras is always a time of great feasting, with lots of parties and big family meals. Many French towns and cities have magnificent carnival parades.

THE MEANING OF 'MARDI GRAS'

The name 'Mardi Gras' means 'Fat Tuesday' in French. The word 'carnival' comes from the Latin words 'carne vale', which means 'goodbye to meat'.

▼ Villagers in traditional costume at a Mardi Gras parade in Alsace.

Nice Carnival

The biggest carnival takes place every year in the city of Nice (pronounced 'Neece'), on the south coast of France. The streets come alive with brass bands, dancers, fireworks and flower battles.

The highlight of the carnival is always a huge procession of decorated floats, carrying people wearing fancy dress and funny masks. They toss striped boiled sweets, called *berlingots*, into the crowds from the floats. They even throw big chunks of nougat, which is a delicious, chewy white fudge made locally from honey and almonds.

A brightly coloured ▶ carnival float.

Crêpes

Crêpes, or pancakes, are the traditional dish eaten throughout France on Shrove Tuesday. They contain either savoury fillings such as cheese, ham, or seafood, or sweet fillings such as lemon and sugar, chocolate sauce or jam. Crêpes are great fun to make – especially when you try and toss them! Some towns organize pancake-tossing competitions to see who can toss the most pancakes, or who can toss them the highest.

Crêpes

EQUIPMENT

Bowl   Whisk
Sieve   Frying pan

INGREDIENTS
(makes 12 crêpes)

250 g Flour
Pinch of salt
2 Eggs
$\frac{1}{4}$ Litre milk
40 g Melted butter
Caster sugar or jam

Sift the flour and salt into a bowl. Add the eggs, milk and melted butter.

Whisk well, and leave for an hour.

Ask an adult to pour a little of the mixture into a hot, greased frying pan. Cook over a high heat until the underside is golden-brown.

Toss or turn the crêpe over and cook the other side. Dust the crêpes with sugar, or spread with jam. Roll them up and serve.

Ask an adult to cook the crêpe. Don't try tossing the pancake yourself.

Easter

Easter is another important religious festival in France. Most families go to church to remember the resurrection of Jesus Christ.

Good Friday marks the start of Easter and the end of Lent. Since animal products, including eggs, were forbidden during Lent in the past, some regions of France still celebrate Good Friday by making omlettes with freshly laid eggs.

Lent is celebrated with chocolate eggs as well as real ones. People give and receive chocolate Easter eggs as presents.

▼ Children painting hard-boiled eggs for Easter.

A special lunch

After church on Easter Sunday, most families celebrate with a big lunch. Everyone from grandparents to grandchildren gathers for this special lunch, which may have four or five courses and lasts all afternoon. Most families cook a feast of their favourite dishes, or local specialities, accompanied by lots of potatoes and vegetables.

EASTER-EGG HUNTS

Easter-egg hunts are exciting races held on Easter Sunday each year. Children are told that while they are asleep at night, the Easter Bunny hides miniature chocolate eggs around their homes and gardens. In the morning they race to find the most eggs!

◀ Looking for Easter eggs on an Easter-egg hunt.

In mountain areas, roast kid (baby goat) is popular. In Périgord, in western France, many families eat duck. However, the most popular meal at Eastertime is lamb, which is cooked in many different ways. One popular lamb dish from Provence, in southern France, is Provence-style lamb kebabs. The recipe is easy to make and the dish is very tasty (you can find it on the opposite page).

▼ Provence-style lamb kebabs.

Provençe-style Kebabs

EQUIPMENT
Bowl
Wooden spoon
Kebab sticks
Chopping board

INGREDIENTS (serves 4)

½ kg Lamb, cut into
bite-sized cubes

2 Tablespoons olive oil

Pinch of salt & pepper

1 Peeled onion, cut into
bite-sized pieces

1 Green pepper, cut into
bite-sized pieces

Thyme, rosemary and
bay leaves

2 Tomatoes, quartered

Mix the lamb, oil, salt, pepper and
herbs in a bowl. Leave them for
2 hours, stirring occasionally, so that
all the flavours blend together.

Thread the pieces of lamb, tomato,
onion and pepper, one after the other,
on to the kebab sticks.

Place the kebabs under a hot grill for
10 minutes, turning regularly.

Serve immediately on a bed of rice,
with salad.

Always be careful when using a hot grill. Ask an adult to help you.

Food Festivals

Most towns and villages in France hold special food festivals, which celebrate their local produce. There are garlic festivals, wine festivals, plum festivals, oyster festivals... even frog festivals!

Beaulieu-sur-Dordogne is famous for growing strawberries. Its Strawberry Fête in May always has many stalls selling homemade products, such as strawberry jam. Every year, the locals pick as many strawberries as possible and take them to four chefs, who bake an enormous strawberry tart.

GIANT STRAWBERRY TART

One strawberry tart made at the Strawberry Fête in Beaulieu-sur-Dordogne is in the *Guinness Book of Records*. It is the biggest in the world! The tart was made with 850 kilogrammes of strawberries and measured 7 metres across.

▼ This record-breaking strawberry tart is the biggest in the world!

▲ They're off! Snail racing in the Osenbach Snail Festival.

Snail Festival

The highlight of Osenbach's Snail Festival is snail racing. As you know, snails move very, very slowly, so the villagers try to speed them up by holding lettuce leaves in front of them. As the snails race, spectators try to guess which one will go the fastest. In the evening, everyone enjoys a local delicacy – large, edible snails, served hot with runny garlic butter.

▲ Snails stuffed with parsley and butter, ready to cook.

Lemon Festival

One of France's most famous food festivals is Menton's Lemon Festival, in February, which lasts for two weeks. Menton is in Provence, in the south of France, where the landscape and climate are ideal for growing oranges and lemons.

The Lemon Festival always attracts thousands of visitors from around France. They watch spectacular parades of floats made of oranges and lemons, and eat tangy orange and lemon tarts, jams and ice-creams. In the evenings, it's fun watching the colourful dancing and firework displays. Lemon mousse is a favourite dessert around this time. You can find the recipe on page 28.

Women throwing ▶ sweets from a moving float, in the Menton Lemon Festival parade.

▼ This octopus is made from hundreds of oranges and lemons.

26

Lemon Delight

INGREDIENTS
(serves 2)

50 g Caster sugar
150 g Natural yoghurt
50 g Cream cheese
150 g Double cream
1/2 Lemon

EQUIPMENT

2 Mixing bowls   Whisk
Lemon squeezer   2 Small dishes

Put the sugar and cream cheese in one bowl and mix well. Add about a teaspoon of lemon juice.

Put the cream in another bowl and whisk until it forms firm, white peaks. Fold in the yoghurt.

Add the cream and yoghurt mixture to the sugar and cream cheese. Gently fold together.

Spoon the mixture into two small dishes. Decorate each dish with a slice of lemon and chill in the fridge for 2 hours.

▲ A delicious bean *cassoulet*.

Pig-squealing Festival

One of the strangest festivals in France is the Pig-Squealing Championship at Trie-sur-Baïse, in south-west France. At this festival, local farmers and villagers have a big lunch, where all the dishes contain pork. There are simple ham and sausage dishes, as well as more unusual dishes such as black pudding (made with pigs' blood), *cassoulet* (a tasty casserole of bacon, sausage and beans) and pigs' trotters. After lunch, a competition is held to see who can sound most like a pig!

Glossary

Carnival A festival held in February in most countries, just before Lent.

Casserole A dish made with several ingredients, which are cooked for some time in a covered pot so the flavours blend together.

Chef A cook.

Citrus fruits A family of fruits including lemons, oranges, limes and grapefruits.

Crops Plants that are grown for food, such as wheat, apples, barley and tomatoes.

Dairy products Milk products, such as butter, cream and cheese.

Delicacy A type of food that is considered very special and delicious.

Edible Suitable to be eaten.

Fold If a recipe tells you to 'fold' a mixture, use a tablespoon to fold spoonfuls of the mixture into one another rather than stirring.

Floats Platforms on wheels, which are usually highly decorated and used in carnival processions.

Guinness Book of Records A special book listing all the greatest achievements (the biggest, the fastest, the smallest etc) in the world.

Ingredients All the different foods needed to make a recipe.

Myrrh A substance from trees, which is used in perfume and medicine.

Parades Processions of people, often in costume.

Resurrection When Jesus Christ rose from the dead on Easter Day, after dying on the Cross on Good Friday.

Rind The skin or peel of fruit.

Roman Catholic A Christian religion whole leader is the Pope, in the city of Rome, in Italy.

Savoury The opposite of sweet. Spicy or salty.

Shallots Small purple onions.

Shrove Tuesday The day before Lent begins. In France this day is called *Mardi Gras*.

Photograph and artwork acknowledgements

The publishers would like to thank the following for contributing to the pictures in this book:

Ace 12; Anthony Blake 18, 22; Cephas 7, 8, 9 (top), 9 (bottom), 11 (top), 13 (top), 13 (bottom), 25, 29; Chapel Studios 21; Eye Ubiquitous 5; Getty Images *Title page*, 27; Image Bank 10; Robert Harding *Cover*, 20, 26; Rex Features 6, 24, 25; Trip 15, 16, 17; Wayland Picture Library 5. Fruit and vegetable artwork is by Tina Barber. Map artwork on page 4 is by Hardlines. Step-by-step recipe artwork is by Judy Stevens.

Topic Web and Resources

MATHS
Using and understanding data and measures (recipes).

Using and understanding fractions.

Using and reading measuring instruments: scales.

SCIENCE
Food and nutrition.

Plants in different habitats.

Separating mixtures of materials: sieving and dissolving.

Changing materials through heat.

GEOGRAPHY
Locality study.

Weather.

Farming.

Comparing physical landscapes.

Influence of landscape on human activities: farming and food festivals.

How land is used.

HISTORY
Investigate the different kinds of equipment and utensils used before electricity.

Investigate the different farming methods used over the past century.

Food & Festivals TOPIC WEB

DESIGN AND TECHNOLOGY
Design and make a cereal box.

Design a poster to advertise a food product.

Technology used in food production.

Packaging.

MODERN FOREIGN LANGUAGES
Language skills.

Everyday activities: food.

People, places and customs.

ENGLISH
Make up a slogan to sell a food product.

Write a poem or story using food as the subject.

Write a list of food words and non-food words.

Write a menu you might find in a French restaurant.

OTHER BOOKS TO READ

Celebrating Christian Festivals by Jan Thompson (Heinemann, 1995)

Christianity by John Logan (Wayland, 1995)

Country Insights: France by Teresa Fisher (Wayland, 1996)

A Feast of Festivals by Hugo Slim (Marshall Pickering, 1996)

Festival!: Carnival by Clare Chandler (Wayland, 1997)

Festival!: Easter by Philip Sauvain (Wayland, 1997)

Food Poems by John Foster (OUP, 1993)

GAMES

Multicultural Food Fun: Young children can match food to their country of origin (NES Arnold, Nottingham)

USEFUL ADDRESSES

Catholic Information Service, 74 Gallow Hill Lane, Abbots Langley, Herts WD5 OBZ

France House, Digbith Street, Stow-on-the-Wold, Gloucestershire GL54 1BN (Tel: 01451 870871) have a wide selection of books, tapes, videos, posters and maps of France.

Index

Page numbers in **bold** mean there is a photograph on the page.